YEMOJA

DRAMA

Kraftgriots

Also in the series (DRAMA)

YEMOJA

DRAMA

Ahmed Yerima

kraftgriots

Published by

Kraft Books Limited
6A Polytechnic Road, Sango, Ibadan
Box 22084, University of Ibadan Post Office,
Ibadan, Oyo State, Nigeria
✆ 234 (2) 8106655
E-mail: kraftbooks@yahoo.com
krabooks@onebox.com

First published 2002

ISBN 978–039–066–9

= KRAFTGRIOTS =
(A literary imprint of Kraft Books Limited)

First printing, July 2002

Computer typeset on 10 point charter typeface by
MOWA COMPUTERS, Ibadan

For

Abdul-Malik
My son, who came with the crowning glory
of Yemoja's blessings.

Author's Note

The story of Yemoja is a celebration of the river goddess. It is a self-conceived myth and it is my attempt at explaining the spread of the worship of the river goddess, from the Yoruba cosmology into the entire diaspora.

The play allows the audience to conceive the gods in the imagery of active aesthetic metaphors of human social preoccupations. It places the Yoruba hero-gods against the barrier of time and within the historic pattern of the traditional and religious rites. The time of existence and their allocations appear temporarily dislocated in the play. The story endows the gods with human feelings, frailties, and attitudes. Therefore, the essence of the hero-gods becomes the essence of man.

In the process of demythologisation, I have again created new Yoruba chant songs or oriki. I have also relied on scholars such as Olu Daramola and A. Jeje in their book *Awon Asa Ati Orisa Ile Yoruba,* C.L. Adeoye and Adeola Yusuff-Badmus. My sincere thanks go to S.A. Odekanyin of the Federal Department of Culture, and Adeola Yusuff-Badmus my consultants.

Ahmed Yerima
Lagos.

Dramatis Personae

1. Orunmila
2. Obatala
3. Esu
4. Ogun
5. Sango
6. Yemoja
7. Iyaji
8. Crier
9. Asipa
10. Balogun
11. Olohun-iyo (Voice)
12. Priestesses of Yemoja — 8 Chorus
13. Ogun Hunters — 5
14. Sango Dancers — 5
15. Obatala's Dancers
16. Drummers and Musicians
17. Egungun
18. Sangodele
19. Littie Girl Dancer

Yemoja

An abridged version of the play was Nigeria's entry at the 29th Festival International Cervantino, Mexico from 10–28 October, 2001. It was performed by the National Troupe of Nigeria with the following cast.

Yemoja	—	Clarion Chukwura-Abiola
Ogun	—	Jahman Anikulapo
Esu	—	Tunji Sotimirin
Orunmila	—	Yemi Adeyemi
Obatala	—	Ojo Rasaki-Bakare
Sango	—	Kayode Idris
Olohun-Iyo/Hunter	—	Olalekan Sobaloju
Oya/Worshipper	—	Taiwo Adeyemo
Asipa/Hunter	—	Husseini Shaibu
Balogun/Alagemo	—	Abiodun Ayoyinka
Iyaji	—	Ayo Ewebiyi
Hunter/Omo-Awo	—	Ahmed Aliu
Hunter/Worshipper	—	Josephine Igberaese
Hunter/Labala Masquerade	—	Opeyemi Raji
Sango's Wife/Worshipper	—	Funke Ajibaiye
Sango's Wife/Worshipper	—	Ojevwe Egbele
Worshipper	—	Chinyere Ekoh
Drummers	—	Lawrence Etim
	—	Adeleke Onanuga
	—	Hunpe Hunga
	—	Elijah Aworinde
	—	Abiodun Ayoyinka
	—	Ahmed Aliu

Dark stage. A bulky, short, half-clad town-crier comes on stage. He wears only a short kembe without a top. He has no shoes on and a clean-shaven head. He carries a small gong, which he beats to the rhythm of his walk. As he beats, the villagers come in twos and threes until there is a crowd gathered.

CRIER: Oba ló rán mi
    Mo tún tidé.
    Ọba ló rá n mi,
    Tí kìí bá se àsẹ Ọba,
    Àní Ọba ló rán mi,
    Mo lè subú,
    Mo lè tàkìtì
    Mo lè jókó
    Mo lè dìde dúró
    Àní Ọba ló rán mi.

    Mo lè jí oníbodè
    Mo lè jí aráalé.
    Àní Ọba ló rán mi
    Ẹnu mi ò lé dùn,
    Tí kìí bá se àsẹ Ọba.
    Àní Ọba ló rán mi.

VILLAGER: Haa! It is the Fat Toad that the Oba sent to talk to us.
(The villagers laugh poking fun at the crier.)

CRIER: Yes, it is the Fat Toad.
    Yes, call me the Fat Toad,
    Laugh all you can, and I will thank Kabiyesi for it.
    Who here does not envy me for
    eating the leftovers of the king?
    (Breaks into a dance)

Ẹma gún iyán Ọba kéré o,
Ẹma gé ẹran Ọba kéré o,
Àwa ọmọ Baba nbẹ,
Awa ná re
Ẹma gún iyan Ọba kéré o,
Ẹma gé eran Ọba Kéré o.

VILLAGER: Please, say what you have to say, and leave us alone. It is a hot night and we have to sleep early.

VILLAGER: We have farms to go to tomorrow morning. We have no king to feed us like the Fat Toad.

CIRER: Ẹ̀tanú,
Jealousy!
The kabiyesi said ... he said.

VILLAGER: Huuhumm!

CRIER: Wait, I must first call on my benefactor.

Kábíyèsí,
Àkànbí,
Ọmọ Àjíílé òpó,
Òpómúléró,
Àkánbí mi,
Ọba a-múlúú dùn,
Ológun ìlú,
Tí n di ilé di ọnà
Ọmọ Oòduà,
Ọmọ Yemoja,
Ìyà ọlọ́mọ wẹ́wẹ́
Yemoja, ore agan
Ó dúró gboin,
Ó fẹ̀hìntì Yemoja,
Ó jókòó rain,

Ó fi Ìyá rẹ̀ ṣẹ ìlérí,
Wọ́n ló sọ̀rọ̀ àìmó.
Ọjọ́ go rí ọ́jọ́,
gbogbo ẹ̀ ló kúkú ṣe.

Àní ta ló sọ pé n ò ní Baba?

VILLAGERS: Kàí oní Baba!

CRIER: Ọba Àkànbí n Babaà mi.

VILLAGERS: Kàí oní Baba!
(The drummers and villagers take over the dance which they all enjoy. The crier watches them for a while.)

CRIER: Enough I say. Ó ti tó!
(Drummers stop.)
I see that you have all taken over the dance of the Fat Toad.
(The dancing and singing stop) I thank you all. Now, the Kabiyesi said that both young and old, both short and tall, both yellow and black, should stay at home tommorow, the day of *awo,* the week of Orunmila by the mouth of the riverside. He wishes to remember his mother, he wishes to appease his mother, Yemoja. The festival begins tonight!

VILLAGER: Háà! I had forgotten.

VILLAGERS: Ha! Àdìsá, how can you forget?

CRIER: How can he not forget, when his two wives have eight children? Between the palm-wine and his wives, he will forget that his aged mother needs to be sunned, like his aso oke dress. Omugo lasan, lasan. And he laughed the loudest when I was called the Fat Toad. You skinny husband of ugly baboons.

11

VILLAGER: Howu! What did he say to deserve such abuses from you?

CRIER: He laughed when I was abused also. Go home all of you, forgetful fools! Yemoja watches over you, giving you children and good harvest. And you say that you forgot the mother who never forgets her own. Go home you ungrateful ingrates.

VILLAGER: The Fat Toad is at his best tonight. His foul breath is as bad as his rotten abuses. Fat ·Toad, the voice of the king, go and sleep, we have heard you.

CRIER: I have said my own.
Go home and prepare for the festival.
Go and prepare for Yemoja's feast.
Bring out your best dresses.
Cook your best food.
The barren come out with your supplications.
The have-nots, bring out your empty bowls.
The festival of the kind mother is here.
The festival of the great goddess is tonight!
Yemoja is here tonight!

(The drums begin to beat to his initial rhythm. Both crier and villagers dance out.)

Ọba ló rán mi
Mo tún tidé
Ọba ló rán mi ò,
Ẹnu mǐ ò leèdùn
Tí kǐî bá se àsẹ Ọba,
Àní Ọba ló rán mi.

(As they dance off, lights go off on stage.)
Dark stage.

Lone voice of singer in the dark. Backstage.

LEAD SINGER: Yemoja!

CHORUS: Emanja!

LEAD SINGER: Yemoja!

CHORUS: Emanja!
(Gangan drums break into slow rhythm.)

LEAD SINGER: Yemoja, gbà mí o.

CHORUS: Bá mi se tèmi.

LEAD SINGER: Ọrẹ́ àgàn gbà mi o.

CHORUS: Bá mi se tèmi.

LEAD SINGER: Ìyá ọlọ́mọ wẹ́wẹ́, gbà mí o.

CHORUS: Bá mi se tèmi.

LEAD SINGER: Òòsa odò, gbà mí o.

CHORUS: Bá mi se tèmi.

LEAD SINGER: Òòsà odò, gbà mí o.

CHORUS: Bá mi se tèmi.

LEAD SINGER: Aya aginjù, gbà mí o.

CHORUS: Bá mi se tèmi.

(As the song is sung at the background, dim light on stage falls on the shrine of Yemoja, a rafia thatched roof on four sticks as stand. There are three pots in the thatched hut. Still in dim light, three priestesses of Yemoja dance out. Two carry pots of water, while one carries a broom. The two pour their water into the three big pots, while the third sweeps the shrine and its

13

surrounding. All the while, slow music and song continue as the three priestesses sway in rhythm with the song.

When the shrine is ready, the gangan drums change into a faster beat. Eight priestesses dance out led by the Iyaji or chief priestess. As they come in the Iyaji leads in the chant.)

ÌYAJÌ: Yemoja, pẹ̀lẹ́ eléwì odò
   Ìyá ọlọ́mọ wẹ́wẹ́
   Yemoja ọ̀rẹ́ àgàn
   A gbé ìyàwó má se àna
   A pa ẹkọrọ yí ìlú ká
   Ọ̀rọ́ọ́rọ́ọ́ a rọ́ ọmọ sí ìté
   A jẹ̀ osinsin máà dá gbèsè
   Ni Oròkí ní n kí ọ sí
   Àbí ní Odegun ni
   Aláwòyè bá mi wo tèmi
   Ọ̀rọ̀ tí í wo ọmọ tí í wo ìyá
   Òrẹ́ àgan báwo ni tèmi
   Ágba ma jumu alásẹ òkúta
   Ọ̀gbon-in gbọ̀-in ra ọmọ bí òkè
   Ọ̀tẹ́tẹ́ ọmọ a tẹ́ lẹ́yìn bí òkè
   A jí pa eléte
   A se ọ̀bùn gba aayo
   Ìlàrè jùmọ̀ bí si ayé
   Yemoja kò jẹ́ báun
   Bí oniyán kò rí omi gbẹ́kẹ̀lé
   Ọlọ́kà kò lè rokà
   Bí alágbàdo kò lè gún ògì
   Kí a tó pé yóò su ẹ̀kọ
   Èmí ti gbẹ́kẹ̀lé obìrin gidi
   Tí í jé Yemoja

Yemoja ní ìyá ọlọ́mọ
Òrìsà odò ni ìyá àgàn
Yemoja ni yóò bá mi se é
Ọ̀rẹ́ àgàn, sé o mò pé
Èmí kò le è dá a se.

*(The "Bami se temi" song still at the background, the
Iyaji leads the prayers.)*

Yèyé-ọmọ ẹja,
Mother of all mothers
We have come again this year
To pay homage to our mother.
Yemoja, the river goddess
Emanja, the goddess of the sea
We call you.
We beg you.
Come out tonight and bless us
Make this night and this year
good times in our lives.

*(A young priestess comes in with a calabash which she
hands over to the Iyaji)*

Yèyé-ọmọ-ẹja
Here is Ègbo
Your favourite food of white corn
Yemoja, accept our offer
And grant us our wishes tonight.

PRIESTESSES: Àsẹ

ÌYAJÌ: Bless all those who have come to help us worship
you.

PRIESTESSES: Àsẹ

ÌYAJÌ: Give the barren children.

PRIESTESSES: Àṣẹ

ÌYAJÌ: Give the young maidens good husbands.

PRIESTESSES: Àṣẹ

ÌYAJÌ: Bless our harvest. Bless the hunters. And bless those in the whiteman's jobs.

PRIESTESSES: Aṣẹ.

ÌYAJÌ: *(Closes her eyes as if in a trance.)*
I can feel it. Yemoja has accepted our prayers.
Yemoja, o kohùn tàwa ọmọ ọ̀ rẹ
Nítorí obì kè é kohùn ọbarìsà
Bẹ́ẹ̀ Sàngó éè kohùn orógbó
Yémoja, gbà a o, kó o jẹ́ wa
Ọdọọdún lẹ̀wà á wà ọ
Ọdọọdún láá mọ́ ọ wà o
Ọdọọdún ni dùndún n dún o
Ọdọọdún ni yóò mọ́ọ dùn fún wa o
Ọdọọdún làá rọ́mọ obì lórí àtẹ o
Ọdọọdún làá mọ́ọ lé síi o

(Wild gangan and bata drums begin. The priestesses dance in a wild frenzy. The young priestess dances too. Iyaji leads the procession off the stage. The young priestess obviously exhausted remains behind. She sits on a wooden log. The flutist and xylophonist play a dirge-like song for Yemoja.

There is the accompaniment of drums and the little girl dances into a frenzy until she falls stepping on a female mask. She picks up the mask, looks round to both sides of the stage while pretending to fling the mask at both the left and the right entrances of the stage. This is a movement which ushers in the dancer who will play the character of Yemoja. The little girl dancer/priestess freezes as the light falls on Ogun in Yemoja's hut. Yemoja dances to meet Ogun.

The drums change to Ogun's beat and Ogun goes into a frenzy. He dances wildly to Yemoja's amusement. She watches for a while.)

YEMOJA: Ògún Lákáayé,
Òsìn-in-mǫlè̩
The man whose eyes melt my heart.
Ogun o, gentle with your feet,
You shall need your strength tonight.
Gentle with your feet.

ÒGÚN: For you, I shall dance forever. For you, I shall break my feet, mend them, and still have a pot full of strength for tonight. Yemoja o, no war can take me tonight. Olówó e̩yǫ mi ò, my love, I promise. Let me dance for you.

I want you perfect, I love you perfect. The way you are forever. Yemoja, let me dance for you.

(Ogun resumes his dance, but when the sound of the talking drum is heard from afar, Ogun stops dancing.)

Oooh, the drums call me

(The drum beats "Ogun I greet you")

ÒGÚN: I greet you too, Ayan.

(The Drum Beats "Ogun there is war")

ÒGÚN: War? Where?

(The drum beats "Ijase")

ÒGÚN: Ha a! So the people of Ijase Oke have not stopped molesting our people? Ha a, odara! It takes three days for the puff-adder to digest a chicken, but on the day of its death, it gets greedy and kills two chickens and attempts to swallaw them both forgetting that they will take longer days to digest and it will also get easily killed by wandering boys. Ayan oo!

(The drum beats "Ho o o")

ÒGÚN: Tell me when do we go to war?

(The drum beats "Tonight")

YEMOJA: Not tonight, Lákáayé.

ÒGÚN: Yes, tonight.

(The chant of war is heard at the background)
They call me already, my Ijala Priests.
Hunters of a thousand demons
Warriors of Ogun.
They call me Yemoja, they call me.

YEMOJA: Ogun, don't look back, I am here with you don't look back.

(From backstage, a voice chants Ogun's praise)

VOICE: Ògún lákáayé, Òsìn-in mọlẹ̀
Ògún aládà méjì
Ó fi ọkan sán ko
Ó fi ọkan yẹ nà
Ọjọ́ Ògún nti orí òkè bọ̀
Àsọ́ iná l'ó mú bọ' ra

Ẹ̀wù èjẹ̀ l'ó wọ
Are ògún ò !

ÒGÚN: He calls me Yeye.
And I am becoming restless.

YEMOJA: Don't leave me, Ogun lákáayé.
Wars last forever, not moments.
Ogun, stay with me tonight.

ÒGÚN: I want to, but, my blood boils.

VOICE: Ògún ò
It is the smell of blood that you like.
Not the smell of a woman's armpit.

YEMOJA: Ogun … warn him. He forgets himself.

ÒGÚN: He calls me Yemoja. War calls a general.

YEMOJA: I call you too, Ogun.
My soft tongue calls you too, Ogun for the sake of
our love, listen to me.

ÒGÚN: But he calls … and as the Are ogun, I must go.
A general does not see war and run or stay at his
lover's side. Yemoja…

VOICE: Ògún ò
Ògún ò
Ògún oní 'lé owó, ọlọ́nà ọlà
Ògún oní 'lé kángunkàngun ọrun
Ó lómi n' ílé f' èjẹ̀ wẹ
Take your bow and arrow
and let us go to war.
Ògún, a won awonna eji
Ẹ̀gbè l'éhìn ọmọ kàn
Ògún méje l'ògún mi

Ògún Alárá ní ìgbà 'jà
Ògún Oníre a gbàgbò
Ògún Ìkòlá a gbà 'gbín
Ògún ...

YEMOJA: Ògún, tell him to shut up.

ÒGÚN: Olóhùn iyò mi ò
Un ò dití mò ngbóhùn un rę.
(Ogun breaks into a dance)
I shall be there
Be there, be there
I shall be there
Where a hundred skulls are bleeding
of cuts from long sharp knives
And fat women are running for shelter
Where the sound of arrows are piercing
feeble bloody chests
I shall be there
Be there, be there
I shall be there.
Yemoja, my true love
one with eyes of ...

YEMOJA: Go, if you must, Ògún,
But don't leave me unprotected.
I was advised you would do this. go Ògún.

ÒGÚN: *(Ogun breaks into a big laugh)*
Is that all?
Howu, Yemoja,
Did you think that Ògún was that heartless?
And leave you unattended?
Never! Ògún's own is always protected.
Èsù my trusted friend will see to that.

He will keep his watchful eyes on my own.

YEMOJA: Ho oo! that devil of a man. Don't call him
Ògún.
I would have liked to remember him in sweeter
terms, but the devil of a man...

ÒGÚN: Èsù is not a devil of a man.
He is the spirit of the devil himself,
His mind, not his strength, is the restless one. Yet he
is a bag of fun. Èsù is my friend, and I love him to
his trickster bones.
Èsù is good, Èsù is my great friend
(Starts Esu's praise chant)

Èsù láàlú Ogiri okoo
Ebora tíí jẹ latopa
O lójú nlẹ̀ fimú sunkún
Ò bélékún n súnkún
Ľáàroye, n s' ẹ̀jẹ̀, laaroye a-fàdá tọrọ epo
Ò bónímímí mí, kẹ̀rù ó bonímímí mi
Latopa n fi gbogbo aramí gúlegúle,
Ẹlékún n sunkún
Láàroye n sẹ̀jẹ̀
Ẹsù láàlú, láàroye, larogo
It is me Ogun calling you,
Esu, my friend.

*(Esu dances in. Slowly at first, then he dances to Ogun.
Both dance in a synchronized movement which ends in
a hug)*

Èsù Láàlú Ẹlẹ́gba ogo
Alámúlamù bàtá
Òrìsà tí ó fẹ́ bàtá kú

Tí n jó bàmùbàmù kiri ilé.
Èsù, it is you that I greet.

ÈSÙ: Ògún Àwóò Awo Olúmòkin are
Awonna-eji, Yannkan-nire
Lakaadijo Osin-mọlẹ̀
A se ègbèfún ẹni tí ó wù ú
koríko odò tí í rú mìnìjọ̀jọ̀
Òrìsà tí alágbẹ̀dẹ n fi obì kàn
Tí ọmọ aráyé n fí ojú di
Ògún ...

ÒGÚN: My friend, it is enough.
You will go on forever if I don't stop you. How is the body?

ÈSÙ: Where I left it this morning. In this thing I call clothes. I am sorry about your mother's death. How are you coping, knowing how close you were to your mother?

ÒGÚN: Fine Esu. Mama's death shattered my trust in life, but I must go on. How is my great friend and your friend Orunmila?

ÈSÙ: He sits there by his diviner's tray awaiting the chance to interpret the mystery of life. Ogun, you did not summon me to ask after Orunmila, what do you want from me?

ÒGÚN: A favour.

ÈSÙ: Then, ask, I have not got all day, there is work to be done.

ÒGÚN: Then, you may leave, because my favour may demand that you tarry a-while. It may demand that you chain your restless nature for a month or two.

ÈSÙ: Already, you punish me. What is it?

ÒGÚN: This is Yemoja. *(Turning to her)*

ÈSÙ: She I know very well. Ogun talk your talk.

ÒGÚN: Yemoja has promised to marry me. But the drums summon me to war. You know the nature of war, it may last a day, or a month, or even a year. Yes, a war is a war. What I want from you is...

ÈSÙ: Yes...

ÒGÚN: Is to help me, as a friend of course, keep Yemoja company until my return. Will you do it, Esu?

ÈSÙ: Consider it done, Ogun.
(Steps towards Yemoja)
Yemoja,
the most precious stone in the oyster's shell
One with skin of pure velvet,
whose eyes melt the most fiery of hearts
Yemoja, it will be my honour to keep you company,
while Ogun is away at war, if you will have me of
course.

YEMOJA: The honour is mine.
Ogun's friend is my friend, Esu.

ÒGÚN: Then, that is done.
Just one more thing, Yemoja.
(Dips his hand into his side bag and brings out a little calabash)
I hope this in your eyes will earn me a deeper love and trust.
I should give this to my mother, but since she is no

23

more, I shall give this to you.

My calabash of life.

You keep it, and keep it very well. Do not open or break it.

You are now my keeper of life,

The keeper of the secret of my strength.

Whenever you miss me strong enough, drop three drops of blood from the neck of a dog on the cover of the calabash and you shall see me.

Keep it with your life.

And whatever you do, do not see the inside of the calabash. Never.

YEMOJA: *(Kneels down to collect it)* I shall guard this with my life.

ÈSÙ: I shall keep an eye on both of them too. Trust me, Ogun.

ÒGÚN: First, I trust you with my precious jewel and my life. Do not let me down brother.

Yemoja, see me to the riverside. I must leave.

ÈSÙ: I shall wait here for you, Yemoja.

Please, wipe your tears and don't cry.

Ogun is a man prone to war, if you cry now, how many more tears will you shed in your entire marital life?

ÒGÚN: Yemoja, you hear that? Wipe your tears and see me to the riverside.

Ogun's own never cries, Yemoja, wipe your tears.

(Dances)

Èmi Ògún ń lọ

Mí ò ro' oko

Mí ò ro' odò
Mò ń re 'bi ogun ìjà ni

I Ogun I am gone
Not to the farm
Not to the river
But to the battlefront.

Èmi Ògún ń lọ
Mí ò ro' oko
Mí ò ro' odò
Mò ń re 'bi ogun ìjà ni

(Both Ogun and Yemoja dance off the stage)

ÈSÙ: *(Watches them dance off stage)*
See them go
hearts locked in what they call love and all I get is
the burden of trust.
Who wants to be trusted?
I hate that word.

So Yemoja is in love with Ogun, is she?
We shall see.
He in turn gives Yemoja his calabash
of life, did he?
We shall see.
And I Esu is to sit and watch over
Yemoja and a stupid calabash, am I?
We shall see.

(Big laugh)
Oh it is all so exciting
I have never stopped desiring Yemoja
But the self-effaced woman won't have me.
As her gaurdian, this is my turn to humiliate her.

Shame her.
Making her the laughing stock she turned me into when she turned down my offer of marriage six moons ago.
I shall pluck her pride and deck her in shameful apparel.
I shall ... ha, here she comes. Gliding gently into my snare.

YEMOJA: Esu, I thank you.

ÈSÙ: What for Yemoja?

YEMOJA: For not telling Ogun about...

ÈSÙ: Us? Ho o! I did not think he should know. It is not good for a man's ego to sing about his disappointments with love. And besides, Ogun has a fiery nature, only his temper knows what he will do if he knew of my earlier intentions to marry you.

YEMOJA: But if he also knew that I turned your offer of love down, I am sure he will understand.

ÈSÙ: Good. He will understand, will he?
(Screams) Ogun lákáayé òsìn-in mọlè!
Ògún ò!
Come! Ògún ò!

YEMOJA: Èsù, what are you doing?

ÈSÙ: Ogun o! Come quickly!
Yemoja wants to explain us to you!

YEMOJA: Èsù, you will kill me first.

ÈSÙ: Ogun will understand, I thought I heard you say.
Let me call him, if we will not see headless bodies

here tonight. Love or no love. Calabash or no calabash.

YEMOJA: That is Ogun. His temper frightens me.

ÈSÙ: His temper? I thought love transcended all that. I was worried about a gentle and beautiful woman like you in love with a man with the temper of a hungry dog. So when I first heard about you and Ogun, I was laughing. I thought it was a funny joke. Until tonight, when I saw you dancing like a sick pepeye about to drown in a puddle of mud.

YEMOJA: Èsù, you taunt me.

ÈSÙ: Taunt you do I? Yemojaa...
There are lovers, and there are lovers.
Some lovers are there, and some lovers are not there.
Yemoja mi o ... I ... Èsù laalu wants to be the lover ... huuhum ... the husband, that is there.

YEMOJA: What do you take me for Èsù? My heart is given to Ogun. You know that.

ÈSÙ: I know that, and I also know that Ogun is not a man who gives his heart to one woman. You heard him, I am his trusted friend, I should know.

YEMOJA: Anyway, my heart is for Ogun.

ÈSÙ: *(Mimicks her)* My heart is for Ogun. Yemoja, grow up and feel the heart of the man you have given yours to. Why do you think his praise-singer says to him when he sings,

Ogun onire, mo ba n ja
Oko ni o se e mi
koriko odo tii ru'binrin toojo-teerun

27

Awonna-eji, Yan'mo n mi,
Alabonle kitikiti
Koriko odo tii ru minimini.

Your Ogun has lovers littered all over the land.
Ilesa, Ondo, Akure, Ekiti, Ile-Ife all over, and most of
them I know and have been body guard to.

YEMOJA: And how many have you also desired?

ÈSÙ: None. None, but you, Yemoja
Yemoja mi o
Eléwì ọdọ̀ tíí bù
Yẹ̀rì yẹ̀rì mo' lote
Tẹ̀lé mi, jẹ́ a relé è mi
Kì n fi ọ́ s'aya à mi

YEMOJA: I shall not go with you, Èsù.

ÈSÙ: *(Pause)* How the hell does he do it? How the hell
does he do it? There you are beautiful, intelligent
and gifted and ready to give all to Ogun. How the
hell does he do it?

YEMOJA: How the hell does he do what, Èsù?

ÈSÙ: I was married once, you know, to a woman I never
met. She was my mother's best friend's aunty's
sister's daughter. She was second in a line of fools. I
did not know her. Our parents married us off with
their mouths long before I could know how to call
my name. She was as ugly as a fat ugly orangutan
with her bosom like a sack of gari. She smelt
constantly of piss. I never knew if she wet her bed,
as I never slept with her for one night. The big joke
is: my wife ran off with her lover, a male baboon the
day after our so-called wedding. She could not stand

my wit, she said. But stupidly, I have never been unfaithful to her. I never thought women even existed until when I met you, and now as always, you turn me down. I still do not know how Ogun does it.

YEMOJA: Ogun does what, Èsù?

ÈSÙ: Have all those women love him in such deplorable ways.

YEMOJA: What women?

ÈSÙ: My lips are sealed
Ẹnu mì kọ lo ó tì gbo ọ́
Ohun Ògún se pèló' obírín
Yemoja, àní ẹnu mí kọ lo ó tì gbọ ó

YEMOJA: Gbó kíni?
Tell me, Èsù.
What must I know about Ogun and his women?

ÈSÙ: Why do you think he gave you his calabash? Why did he tell you never to open it? Why?

YEMOJA: Why? Because he loves me.

ÈSÙ: Go on fool yourself.

YEMOJA: Tell me. I am getting all confused.

ÈSÙ: It is clear that Ogun wants you fooled. If and when you do have the boldness to open the calabash, you will see Ogun at work with all those women. That was why his late mother used to keep it for him.

YEMOJA: Ogun, could this be right? The calabash will help me see him and what he is doing now?

ÈSÙ: With all his women and many more but I shall not

push you any further.

YEMOJA: Say no more, Èsù, my mind is made up.
(She goes into her hut)

VOICE: Èsù, Ọ̀tá Òrìsà
Òsètura l'orúkọ baba mọ̀ ọ́
Alágogo ìjà l'orúko ìyá ńpè ẹ́
Èsù Òdàrà ọmọkùnrin Ìdọ́lọ́fin
Ó lé sónsó s'órí ẹsẹ̀ ẹlẹ́sẹ̀
Kò jẹ, kò sì jẹ́ kí ẹni ńjẹ gbé e mì
A kí í l'ówo láì mú t'Èsù kúrò
Asọ̀tún-sòsì láì ní 'tìjú.
Èsù, àpáta s'ọmọ ọlọ́mọ l'ẹ́nu
Ó fi òkúta dípò iyọ

ÈSÙ: Dá kẹ́ ẹnu rẹ!
I say shut up!
Whatever I do is none of your business, is it?
Gbé ẹnu rẹ sóhùn-ún!

VOICE: Èsù o
A lover to your best friend is like a sister,
Èsù, why?

ÈSÙ: Don't you give me any moral rubbish. I did not force her, did I? I only said she may ... and the woman in her took over, so leave me alone Olohun-iyo.

(Èsù starts a victory dance when Yemoja comes out of the hut with Ogun's calabash. Èsù covers his face as Yemoja opens it. Loud drums as Yemoja falls paralysed in both her left leg and hand. She writhes in pain)

YEMOJA: Yeh ... I am in pain
Èsù, save me. My foot, my arm, I cannot feel any power. Èsù save me.

ÈSÙ: I warned you.

YEMOJA: But you said...

ÈSÙ: Now, don't you quote me wrongly. I never said that you should open the calabash, I said you may...

YEMOJA: Save me all the same.
I am in deep pain. Èsù, save me.

ÈSÙ: I will save you, if you can promise me that once you are well, you shall spend two nights with me.

YEMOJA: Two nights, Èsù, I cannot be unfaithful to Ogun.

ÈSÙ: Then lie there and wait for Ogun.
Ogun mi o
The one with eyes for the perfect Yemoja, our beautiful cripple wants to be your faithful bride.
(Gives a wild cynical laugh)
She wants to be faithful with one leg and one hand.
Yemoja, lie there and wait for Ogun onire.

YEMOJA: Èsù, please, I beg you. I shall stay with you for one night only, please, save me from my shame.

ÈSÙ: One night, that is even enough. You promise?

YEMOJA: I promise, Èsù. By the gods I promise, just cure me of this infliction, and I shall spend that night with you. Save me Èsù, save me!

ÈSÙ: Only one man can save you now. My friend Orisa-nla. Wait let me call him.
Obàtálá mi
Òrìsà ńlà mi
Ikú tí í ba gbé ilé f'Qlá ran 'ni!

Aláse! Ó sọ ẹnìkan soso di igba ènìyàn
Sọmí di' rún sọmí d'igba
Sọmí d'ọ̀tàlé-légbèje ènìyàn
My Orisa bigger than man
That grows every day
My Orisa that grows so big, he cannot be carried.
Banta banta ninu ola
Ó sùn nínú àlà
Ó ti inú àlà dìde
Baba ńlá, ọkọ Yemowo
It is I Èsù,
Obàtálá, I call you.

(Slowly the music of Obàtálá starts. Èsù sways gently to the music as Obàtálá dances in. They both dance)

OBÀTÁLÁ: Èsù láàlú, laaroye, larogo
Ògògó onímú erin
Òbúngú, òbángá, òbúngú,
Elẹ́sẹ̀ kan, baara tí í jẹ́
latopa, I greet you

ÈSÙ: Òrìsà ńlá Adìmúlà
Olójúlu kára bí ajere
Òbàbá arúgbo
Òrìsà gbìngbinnìkìn
I greet you, too.

OBÀTÁLÁ: Why does Èsù disturb me at this time of the day?

ÈSÙ: To call on the favour you owe me.

OBÀTÁLÁ: Èsù, you never fail to amaze me. The favour is six years old.

ÈSÙ: A favour is a favour, Obàtálá. Look down and see

32

why I called you at this time of the day.

OBÀTÁLÁ: Ha! This is Yemoja.

YEMOJA: It is me, Orìsà àlà. Save me.
Save me from this painful infliction.

OBÀTÁLÁ: I shall do my best, Yemoja.

ÈSÙ: Do your best, and I shall reward you with the gift
of a white horse.

OBÀTÁLÁ: Her beauty gratifies my work. I can feel her
kind and gentle nature call my spirits.

YEMOJA: I am grateful. On my part, I shall give...

ÈSÙ: Nothing more shall be needed after the gift of the
white horse. We must not spoil Obàtálá's kind spirits.

OBÀTÁLÁ: Nothing shall be needed at all. *(Holds her)*
Where do you feel the pain?

YEMOJA: All over, especially my foot and left hand. It is
as if a bolt of oily fire poured on them. Save me from
the pain.

OBÀTÁLÁ: Save your strength. I shall need some leaves
and freshly fetched water from the pond.

ÈSÙ: I shall go fetch the water.

OBÀTÁLÁ: Go quickly, we must not allow the poison eat
the flesh to the bones. Go quickly, Èsù.

ÈSÙ: I am off, Obàtálá. I beg you, nothing must happen
to her.
(Exit Èsù)

OBÀTÁLÁ: *(Picks up his bag, opens it, brings out some*

medicine and begins to rub on Yemoja's leg)
This will hurt a little, but the real cure will start when
Èsù returns with the water. How does it feel?

YEMOJA: Soothing, my lord.

OBÀTÁLÁ: Good. Let me pluck the leaves I need.
(Exit to the back of Yemoja's hut)

ÈSÙ: *(Èsù returns with a small calabash of water)*
Where is Obàtálá?

YEMOJA: Behind the house.

ÈSÙ: I have brought the water.

YEMOJA: Thank you.

ÈSÙ: You look better already. I knew that Obàtálá could
do it. *(Obàtálá comes in with a handful of freshly cut
leaves)* I have come with the water.

OBÀTÁLÁ: Good. Help me take her in. I cannot work in
the open. *(Goes to Yemoja)* We have to move you in.

YEMOJA: Do whatever you want with me. Just cure me,
Òrìsà àlà, cure me.

OBÀTÁLÁ: *(Both men carry Yemoja into the hut, Èsù
comes back to take Obàtálá's bag and calabash of
water into the hut. He comes back out of the hut,
worried.)*

ÈSÙ: Èsù láàlú!
You have done this one
O ti se eléyìí nó
Wàá sè mî
(Pause) I think she is mine
(Does a dance of victory)

34

Did you hear how she said that she was grateful to me?
Did you not see how her eyes lit up to me? My one night awaits her gratitude.
Èsù, prepare yourself for love at last. I can feel the evening breeze ready to spread the tale of coming adventure. After one night, she will be mine forever. For I shall tell even the worms of my conquest. Yemoja, I have fooled you this time. Èsù, I say you have done this one.
Ma de se mi
(Yemoja lets out a scream)
Practise the scream Yemoja, you shall need the voice loud and clear when we spend the nights together.
I wish my mother could see me now. I used all my wits, and Yemoja is mine.
My mother would have been proud of me today. Èsù, ani wa se mi.
(Yemoja lets out another scream)
Gently with her Obàtálá
Beautiful women should be handled gently,
Gentle with her.
(Yemoja lets out a loud laugh)
What is he up to now?
Why is she laughing?
She should be in pain. *(Pause)* I hope...
Could it be...
Would Obàtálá try...

Can Yemoja be so cheap?
Could she have fallen for Obàtálá's gentle touch?
She should be in pain
Not laughing ... at what?

At me? … haa Èsù at you?
Am I the figure for their jokes now?
Did you not see her eyes when I returned from the
pond? … how … they hardened at my person and
how…
her pupils fell gently on Obàtálá
No not yet. I shall wait.
I can wait … I have to wait.
There is always a way out
If she turns me down now,
then she will feel the weight of Èsù.
I can love passionately, and yet I can
hate with equal tempo. Don't try me woman!
(He peeps into the hut)
Ha Obàtálá massages her naked leg and she enjoys
it.
My ego crashes, crumbles again,
and I am in pain, yet, she enjoys it.
(Peeps again)
I have seen enough
My tongue grows dry, and my eyes grow green,
then Ogun shall hear all from my tongue.
Obàtálá orisa'ala you pour oil on your
white dress and the drums beat your shame
Obàtálá you have bitten what you can
not chew, but if you insist, then
chew with caution for I shall line
your teeth for sale at the
market square.
Èsù, now the line is drawn
Obàtálá wants your wicked side
I think he grows weary of his dull colour
swift with your legs, Èsù Laalu

there is work to be done.
Let me colour his white in shame.

(Lights go off)

Battlefront. Ògún is wounded with a wrapped bandaged hand. He is with two other war generals when lights come on. There is a war chant when lights come on.

ÒGÚN: Asípa, your men came on too early. They should have come from the left.

ASÍPA: I think the people of Ijase must have used witchcraft on them. I personally gave them a specific time to attack.

ÒGÚN: Now see what their wrong decision did to me. Before my soldiers were ready, we had the enemies on us. We lost too many men when it was not neccessary.

BALÒGÚN: Our judgement was right, but I do not understand why my men suddenly grew weak.

ÒGÚN: For one second, as we ran down the hill, there was a little cloud, then from nowhere I felt dew falling on me.

BALÒGÚN: Dew, my lord?

ASÍPA: It was a very hot afternoon.

ÒGÚN: Hot afternoon indeed, but from nowhere, I felt the early morning dew, and a weakness all over. My limbs were in pain, and my eyes refused to see clearly, something was wrong. My strength just left my body and walked away. Something bad was in the air. Then came this little boy with his spear and with little effort, he pierced the shoulder of Ògún.

ASÍPA: I am sorry, my lord. We have since beheaded him.

ÒGÚN: Where was my protection? *(Thoughtful)* Could

it be ... that, no ...

ÈSÙ: Ògún Ò
      Şo n 'gbóhùn ẹnu mi
      Ẹ̀bẹ̀ ni mo nbẹ̀ ọ́
      Ilé ti dàrú o ló n jagun
      Mo gbalé, gbodó, Mo gbokoogi loo wà
      Ògún níí dá gbáú bí 'igi dá
      Ògún n lelénmọ̀ okùnrin
      Ikú tí i forí i jà, tí í fìrù jà
      Ìfẹ́ rẹ̀ ti i dàrú

ÒGÚN: Èsù, what are you doing here?

ÈSÙ: I am here to defend my friend's honour.

ÒGÚN: What do you mean, Èsù?

ÈSÙ: *(Sees the bandaged shoulder)* Yee pa ripa! So it has
      happened already? I warned her, I begged her, but
      she won't listen. How does the pain go?

ÒGÚN: What happened?

ÈSÙ: She meant to have you killed, ha! Yemoja, see what
      you have done to a man you say you love.

ÒGÚN: Èsù, I say what happened?

ASÍPA: Talk to us quick, we are in the middle of a war.

ÈSÙ: It is Yemoja and Obàtálá.

ÒGÚN: Yes, what happened?

ÈSÙ: I was seated keeping an eye on Yemoja when I saw
      Obàtálá with her promising her his love forever. I was
      shocked, Obàtálá is not one for womanising. I think
      Yemoja charmed him.

ÒGÚN: Charmed him? Huumhum, so Obàtálá wants to eat from my cooking pot, does he?

BALÒGÚN: Eewo, he who plays with Ògún, plays with his death.

ÈSÙ: She had charmed him, the way he charmed you. And then I heard Obàtálá tell her to open your calabash of life, I knew danger was going to befall you at the battleground.

ÒGÚN: It did. Danger came. There was a smoke of weakness all over. I lost brave men, Èsù, I lost great warriors, all because of Yemoja. She will pay for this. They shall both pay.

ÈSÙ: That was why I came, to tell you, so that they can pay dearly for their betrayal of your trust.

ÒGÚN: They shall, Èsù, they shall. Where are they now?

ASÍPA: Let me take some men there, and kill them myself, my lord.

ÒGÚN: No, their heads belong to me.

ÈSÙ: I left them in Yemoja's house. They were so entangled; they did not see me until I left them to come here.

(Ògún gets up, and in a wild movement begins to dance his war dance)

BALÒGÚN: My lord, let me go with you.

ASÍPA: Yes, my lord, you are not too strong, let Balògún go with you.

ÒGÚN: *(Still dancing)* No this is my fight. You stay and

fight the war. I shall join you by the evening. Èsù, let us go.

(Exit Ògún. Èsù follows but stops when he hears the voice of Olohun-Iyo)

VOICE: Ògún, máàjó ijó ẹtẹ́
    Ògún, máàjó ijó ẹtẹ́
    Ijó ẹtẹ́ ni ijó Èsù
    Ògùn, máàjó ijó ẹtẹ́

    Ògún, do not dance the dance of shame
    Ogún, do not dance the dance of shame
    Èsù wants you to dance the dance of shame
    Ògún, do not dance the dance of shame.

ÈSÙ: Olóhùn-iyò shut up!

(Lights go off sharply)

Yemoja's hut. Both Yemoja and Obàtálá are outside the hut. Yemoja is excited, Obàtálá seats watching her and also eating, Yemoja brings him palm-wine, Obàtálá is obviously pleased with himself.

OBÀTÁLÁ: You will kill me with this delicious meal, Yemoja.

YEMOJA: I am so happy, I could sing and dance at the same time. Orisa'ala, I thank you.
Òrìsà'ala mi ò
Baba ńlá mi ò
Bàntà banta nínú ọlá
Okòrin gbìgìgbà
Ibi rere ni Obàtalálá kalẹ̀
Òrìsa ńlá òsèeré mágbò
Obàtálá mú nú mi dùn
sọ mí lẹ́kún do'yin.

OBÀTÁLÁ: You flatter me, Yeye.

YEMOJA: You flatter me with happiness.
If I had the powers, I would have given you a new wife myself, but Yemowo will kill me.

OBÀTÁLÁ: She will. And the joke is, I won't even know what to do with a new wife, unless she can cook as good as you.

YEMOJA: Then, why don't I follow you myself?

OBÀTÁLÁ: Ògún will kill me. *(They both laugh)*

YEMOJA: Drink the wine, it is very fresh.

OBÀTÁLÁ: It is too strong. It is good palm-wine only for Ògún. If I take a sip, I will dance all night, and forget to go home.

YEMOJA: Very good. That is what I like in a man. A man who can dance, is in tune with the gods. Obàtálá, dance for me.

OBÀTÁLÁ: I cannot. I will rumple my dress.

YEMOJA: Stain your dress with my oil
Rumple your dress with my dance
Fire your spirits with my wine
Give me joy with your feet
Dance for me Obàtálá
Mú nú mi dù, Obàtálá
jó fún mi, Òrìsà'àlà
Dance.

OBÀTÁLÁ: I cannot.

YEMOJA: Then I must turn away knowing now that Obàtálá does not share in my joy.
Obàtálá does not want me happy.
You bruise my pride Orisa nla.
(Pretends to sulk)

OBÀTÁLÁ: No, stop it. See. Okay one sip.
(He raises the calabash to his lips, Yemoja tilts it and Obàtálá drinks a lot more than he intended.) Woman, you will choke me. Haa my eyes are heavy all of a sudden.

YEMOJA: Then, dance for me.

OBÀTÁLÁ: I cannot, but the wine tells me to.

YEMOJA: Do it. Obàtálá, do it.

OBÀTÁLÁ: My feet move on their own, Yeye.

YEMOJA: Let them. Don't stop them.

OBÀTÁLÁ: Then, hold my hands. Help me up.

YEMOJA: *(Holds his hands)* They are cold.

OBÀTÁLÁ: It is the wine.

YEMOJA: Then, dance out the cold. Dance for me Orisa nla, dance for me.

(Ògún and Èsù come in, see them and hide watching Obàtálá and Yemoja holding each other. Ògún wants to run on stage, Èsù holds him back. The music starts and both of them begin to dance. Obàtálá dances wildly, drunk and almost falls when Yemoja grabs hold of him. With Obàtálá in Yemoja's arms Ògún comes in angry.)

ÒGÚN: *(Ògún can no longer control himself, he jumps on stage wildly. Breaking them up he brings out his sword and is about to kill Obàtálá but Èsù and Yemoja hold him back.)* Prepare to meet Olodumare today.

OBÀTÁLÁ: Ògún, you choke me.

ÈSÙ: Ògún, not now.

ÒGÚN: You saw them, did you not?

ÈSÙ: I did. But not now, not this way.

ÒGÚN: What other way does one destroy a usurper? Obàtálá, I shall kill you today.

YEMOJA: Please, Ògún, it is not what you think. *(Tries to hold him)*

ÒGÚN: Don't touch me, woman. First him, then, I shall deal with you later. And to think I thought we could be married.

YEMOJA: It is not what you think, Ògún. Leave him alone, don't kill him. Control your temper.

ÈSÙ: Huum, Ògún this is not the way to kill a man who is drunk. I think there is a better way to kill him. In front of everybody. Oh! I cannot begin to think of the shame. It is the market day in two days' time. In front of everybody, you can kill both of them. That way, you will drive fear into the hearts of all men who dare to cross your path now and in the future.

ÒGÚN: Good. *(Relaxes his grip on Obàtálá)* I shall in two days' time unmask you to your shame at the market square. We shall meet for a fight to the end. And when you meet Olodumare, tell him that you dared to fish in Ògún's water and got drowned in your blood. Obàtálá, in two days' time, Ògún shall beat the drums and you still drunk in your foolery, shall dance with your lover, the dance of shame.

(As Ògún and Èsù exit, lights go off)

Orunmila is seated in his hut. He is consulting Ifa when Yemoja comes in.

YEMOJA: Babaà mi
    Òrúnmìlà ni Babaà mi
    Ojọ́ nbá fẹ́é tẹ́
    Òrúnmìlà ni Babaà mì
    Baba tí kìí ba ọmọ rẹ̀ yodì
    Ta ni ńbá sá lòóbá?
    Àní Òrúnmìlà ni Babaà mi
    Ta ni n' bá sunkún lò óbá?
    Àní Òrúnmìlà ni Babaà mi
    Wọ́n ní Yemoja rìn síta
    Wọ́n fẹ́ ba orúkọ mìi jẹ́
    Wọ́n fẹ́ da epo sí aṣọ àlà mi
    Moróhuntólú, Mosiakáràbà,
    Ọmọ okinkìn tí í mérin fọn
    Ọmọ èékánná ọwọ́ ko j'ekun o ara abẹ
    Ọmọ olobe tó fi orí jó adé to mọ odi umo jimo
    O mà jíire lónì o

ÒRÚNMÌLA: Yemoja, mo jí re loni. My daughter. You are welcome. I have seen it all.

YEMOJA: Then, you have heard how Ògún accused me wrongly. How he claims that I threw myself cheaply at Obàtálá.

ÒRÚNMÌLA: I heard it all, Yemoja, you must be patient.

YEMOJA: Baba, how can I be patient when Ògún has already soiled my name? The whole town is singing that Yemoja has put her leg in the bush. I will not take this, Baba. I shall fight him with all my strength.

ÒRÚNMÌLA: My daughter, when I first heard of your

relationship with Ògún, I wondered how a cool spirited girl like you would have something to do with a hot iron like Ògún.

YEMOJA: He dances well, Baba. It was at Oya's feast. The feast she gave after her illness. He had taken so much palm-wine. That day, he danced and danced until the drummers were tired and half their drums torn. His fast feet almost did not touch the ground. Ayan called him, and he answered his every sound. I liked him instantly...

ÒRÚNMÌLA: And now...

YEMOJA: His name? I cannot stand the mention of his name, Baba. His name turns my stomach. I cannot marry a man who is quick of temper. He has no mind of his own. Èsù is his best friend. Jooro-jaara-jooro, he pushes him.

ÒRÚNMÌLA: Women remain the greatest wonder of Olodumare's gift to the world. Yemoja...

YEMOJA: Baba...

ÒRÚNMÌLA: What do you want from me?

YEMOJA: I want you to stop him, Baba. In two days' time, Ògún plans to disgrace me at the market-square.

ÒRÚNMÌLA: Tell me, Yemoja, is Obàtálá innocent?

YEMOJA: Baba, I swear by Olodumare, Obàtálá means nothing to me. He was kind to me and I showed him hospitality in return, that was all, Baba.

ÒRÚNMÌLA: Obàtálá ... O ní wà tútù tí ńkó jògbòn kiri ... Haaa ... this will be the fifth time this year that I will have to save him from being wrongly accused. I have told him people often misunderstand his kindness, but he never listens to me, Obàtálá...

YEMOJA: Baba, help him. Don't let Ògún drag his name into Èsù's shameful mud.

ÒRÚNMÌLA: Ìwọ náàgan, oníjọ̀gbọ̀n ni ọ́
Ò ńfi ẹwà re da ìlú rú.

Your beauty gives me a headache, Yemoja.

YEMOJA: It is not my fault, Baba. If Olodumare decides to give me my beauty, I cannot help it, if men cannot control themselves. Baba, do what I have begged you to and leave my beauty alone.

ÒRÚNMÌLA: Wait. *(He consults Ifa. Yemoja is anxious)*
Esinsin a máa kun orí ìmi woinwoin;
T' o lógún ẹrú, t' ó ní òun kò lẹ́nìyàn.
Esinsin a máa kun orí imi woinwoin,
Ò dá f'ódù mẹ́rìndínlógún
T'ó l' ójì ìwọ̀fà tó ní òun kò lénìyàn
T'ó bá jé pé ti òun;
Òun Òrúnmìla
Odo a jẹ́ ki nwọn máa bá òun do
Ibi ti àdàbà bá ti d' ọjà sí
Ni ẹyẹ oko ti í ná a
Ibi ti ọgẹ̀dẹ̀ bá ti fi ìdí balè sí
Ìgbo ní i dà
Ibi tí ìkòkọ̀ bá ti fi ìdí balè sí
Igbó ní í dà
Èwòn mẹ́rìndínlógún ni nwọ́n nfara wọn
Iré t'ìhín wá, ire t'ọ̀hun bọ̀
Ajere olonona.

Ire t' ìhín wá, ire t' òhun bò
Ajere olonona.

My daughter, I see it all. I see your "okiki" spreading throughout the world. I see men and women, boys and girls, black and white all singing and dancing for Yemoja.

YEMOJA: When, Baba?

ÒRÚNMÌLA: Ire t'ìhín wá, ire t'òhun bò
Ajere olonona
Ire t'ìhín, wá, ire t'òhun bò
Ajere olonona

A time not too long from now, Yemoja.
I see you in a river...
YEMOJA: Baba, this is my dream.
I saw myself in the deep blue sea
And all the fishes and wonders of the sea swimming along with me.
For days, I remained under the sea
No food, no water except the sweet music of the fins of the fishes and the clicks of the claws of the lobsters and crabs. When I got tired I would climb the back of big giant turtles.
They all heard my language and I was one with them.
And when my eyes were dazed with sea water, I raised my head, and behold
I saw the world full of peoples all dressed in white, dancing and singing my name.
Baba, this is my dream, what mystery does the deep blue sea hold for me?

ÒRÚNMÌLA: *(Consults Ifa)*

Huum, Yemoja mi, there is a journey you must embark upon.

YEMOJA: When, Baba?

ÒRÚNMÌLA: I cannot see that now, but the smell of the sea is strong, and the dress gets very wet. Soon Yemoja, soon.

YEMOJA: Look closer, Baba, I must know.

ÒRÚNMÌLA: Há à. Ó ti yé mi.
Yemoja, the spirit of your peoples call you.
Yemoja, the peoples need their mother,
Yemoja, the peoples need children, joy and happiness.
Yemoja, the peoples need you.

YEMOJA: I shall give them whatever they want if only you will promise me that you shall avert the shame Ògún plans for me in two days' time.

ÒRÚNMÌLA: I cannot promise, Yemoja, but on that day follow your heart.

YEMOJA: Will you follow me there? I shall need a friend.

ÒRÚNMÌLA: That I can promise you. Ògún and Obàtálá in a fight. It puzzles me. Yemoja, I shall be there at least to try and stop the fight from taking place.

YEMOJA: Baba, I shall be most grateful. One more thing, Baba...

ÒRÚNMÌLA: Yes Yemoja...

YEMOJA: Tell me more about my journey...

ÒRÚNMÌLA: *(Consults Ifa)*

It is now clearer. In two days' time, you must...

(Lights fade)

Sàngó's courtyard. Sàngó is trying to teach his son, Sàngódélé how to fight with his axe.

SÀNGÓ: Raise your axe up, son. Keep your eyes always on your enemies. Do not shake your hand. Straight and aim for the neck or the chest. Those are the weakest points. Do you understand?

SÀNGÓDÉLÉ: I understand, father, but Baba mi, I do not want to be a warrior.

SÀNGÓ: Èèwọ̀! The son of Sàngó, a weakling? Èèwọ̀. Raise up the axe or I shall cut off your head.

SÀNGÓDÉLÉ: *(He obeys, then puts down the axe again.)* Baba mi, I want to be a farmer. All this show of power frightens me.

SÀNGÓ: Tonight, with a knife on the neck of your mother, I shall ask her who your father is. Hold up the axe or I shall split your head in two.

OBÀTÁLÁ: *(Enter Obàtálá)* Sàngó.
My friend
Sàngó èé kọhùn orógbó
Sàngó èé kohùn tàgbò
Òréè mi mọ kohùn-un tèmi
Akáta yẹrìyẹrì
Olúaso a-rékújáyé ee
Listen to the boy
If out of twenty children, one
wants to become a farmer
Sàngó let him be.

SÀNGÓ: Obàtálá
Ẹlẹ́wù àlà
My friend who creates at will

Obàtálá
I greet you.

OBÀTÁLÁ: I greet you too, Sàngó.
But my heart is heavy.

SÀNGÓDÉLÉ: E ka san Baba mi *(He postrates)*

OBÀTÁLÁ: Ka san omo mi,
Sàngódélé olori re,
Omo Sàngó a-rekujaye!

SÀNGÓ: Unburden it my friend,
for Sàngó owes you a favour.
After you cured my wife, Oya,
I swore to do whatever you ask.
Obàtálá, speak to me.

OBÀTÁLÁ: It is Ògún.

SÀNGÓ: What has Ògún done again? I should have
driven him out of the town at the last Egungun
festival, but you did not let me. What has he done
this time?

OBÀTÁLÁ: He has sworn to fight me in two days' time
at the market-square.

SÀNGÓ: Two days' time? Why?

OBÀTÁLÁ: It is a long story, I shall tell you before I go,
but first I must drink some water.

SÀNGÓ: Ó yá, Sàngódélé, get some water for my friend,
and tell your mother that we have one more mouth
for lunch.

OBÀTÁLÁ: I shall not be able to wait for lunch. I say
Ògún wants to stain my white robes. First, he accuses

me of stealing his lover, Yemoja, and now he says that he will disgrace my person at the market square.

SÀNGÓ: *(Gives a big laugh)* I set my trap and the antelope says he would rather camp there for the night. Obàtálá, just to avoid taking you for granted, tell me what you want from Sàngó.

OBÀTÁLÁ: Sàngó
A bínú làálàá
A dínú làálàá
Sàngó mi ò
Má'jẹ́ kí Ògún dójú tìmí
Aṣọ àlà ni mo wọ̀
Sàngó mi ò
A benugan-an mi ò
Gbà mí lọ́wọ́ ẹtẹ́

SÀNGÓ: It is done then. In two days' time I shall fight Ògún in your name. And if I defeat him, Yemoja shall be yours.

OBÀTÁLÁ: No, you can keep her. I am content with my only wife, Yemowo. Two women will kill me.

SÀNGÓ: As you wish. There is always room for more in my house.

OBÀTÁLÁ: Sàngó…

SÀNGÓ: And now that you are here, you must do something about that Sàngódélé. Sàngó cannot have a whimp for a son. It will kill me first to see my own son digging the earth instead of stabbing at the heart of his enemies.

OBÀTÁLÁ: If you insist then I shall give him some

medicine. But can he swallow the raw heart of a hen?

SÀNGÓ: I will make him swallow the raw whole head of a bull if I have to.

OBÀTÁLÁ: It is done then. I shall start work after lunch.

SÀNGÓ: Now, tell me what really happened?

OBÀTÁLÁ: You see, it all started with Èsù…

(Lights go off)

Full lights on stage. Music and Egungun performing. The villagers are there to cheer the crowd. The villagers stand behind six arranged stools. There is the biggest stool. Seated on it is Òrúnmìla. Yemoja is seated on one, Èsù is seated on one, Obàtálá is seated on one. The remaining two are at the sides and are empty. Òrúnmìla nods to Èsù who rises.

ÈSÙ: Ó ti tó!
I greet you all.

CROWD: We greet you, too.

ÈSÙ: We all know why we are here today. For those who go to places without asking, it is to witness the fight to the end between Ògún lakaaye, Osin-in' mole, and Sàngó Olukoso arekujaye! The fight is not Sàngó's own, but as it is in his character, Sàngó carries another axe for Obàtálá. Yes, go on and ask me what the prize is. *(Turns and points to Yemoja)* There she is, Yeye-ọmọ-ẹja, arẹwa obirin. Eleji pami n'ku, the jewel in the crown of the Gods.

CROWD: Yèyé Ò!
Yemoja O!
Emanja O!
We greet you all.

ÈSÙ: Where is Olohun-iyo?

VOICE: I am here Èsù.
Obeying the intelligent words of my father, Baba lamilami.
He had told me that my voice is a gift
And although, I can massage the ego of the sun,
I can never hurry the sunshine

56

Èsù I can not hurry you
I shall wait until I am called.

ÈSÙ: I have called you Olohun-iyo.

VOICE: I answer Èsù laalu
The one with colours which deceive
the pregnant woman
The one who creates a fight among the newly-wed
The one who allows the aged couple
eat their son, thinking he is an antelope.
Èsù Ọ̀dàlẹ̀ ìlú
Èsù láàlú, n lo laarin epa
Àtàri è rí fíéfíé
Oni lopelope poun ga
laaroye afàda tọrọ epo
Ogiri oko.

ÈSÙ: Ó titó!
Olóhùn-iyò
One with the coated tongue
I say it is enough.

VOICE: Then, let me call on another
whose ears will hear my flatter
Sàngó ò!
Olukòso ò!
Kábíyèsí, Sàngó Àjàláàjí oníbọ̀n ọrun
A bọ́ lu ọmọ bí owú
Ọkọ mi asọ̀ńbọ-conbo idà
Èbìtì ká-wọ́-pọ̀n sèyìn soro,
Èbìtì ká ọwọ ìjà lérí
Eni tí mogbà ń béèrè
Eyí tí yóò se ni à ń wòye

Bí Sàngó o bá wọn jà
Á kọ́ yan lọ bí Ẹdẹ
A kù fisàn fisàn lọ bí Èjìgbò
Kí ó tó dé oníjá á gbàgbé
Ònlàjà á ti sùn ló fọn fọn
Ó bá baálé jẹ iyán ìgángàn
Ó tún pa ọmọ rẹ̀ sójú òde.

ÈSÙ: Olóhùn-iyọ̀
Do not start the fight with your mouth.

Olóògùn ni Sàngó ọkọ Òya
Ó bẹ́ ọmọ lórí kalẹ̀
Ó fi ẹsẹ̀ tiiri rẹ̀ wò
Bírí, bírí ní í jókòó bí ilẹ̀ ọjà
Á ba ọlọ́mọ pínhun
Má gbagbé ọjọ́ tí o dá fún mi
Sàngó, mo pè ọ́
gbó'hùn, ẹnu-ùn mi!

(The Sàngó drums start, his soldiers dance, singing.
Oya comes in carrying his pot of fire. The drums grow
into a frenzy and the dancers also dance wildly until
Sàngó appears. He dances wildly throwing fire from
his mouth. The crowd continue to applaud. Èsù gives
Sàngó a sign and beckons on him to stand on one side
of the crowd. Sàngó does. Olohun-iyo steps forward)

VOICE: Ògún Àwóò, Olúmokin are
Awonna-eji Yannkan-nire
Lakaadijo Òsìn-mọlè
A se ègbè fún ẹni tí ó wù ú
Koríko odò tí í rú mìnìjọ̀jọ̀
Òrìsà tí alágbẹ̀dẹ
Ògún kò riru lágbẹ̀dẹ

Bí ó ti ń kọ ara ilé lóminú
Bẹ́ẹ̀ ni ó n dẹ́rù ba ara oki.
Egúngún olú Ifẹ̀ tí í sán mòrìwò opẹ
Ní ilé ni, lókó ni
Òrò Ògún sòro jọjọ
Ìjà Ògún kò se é rí

ÈSÙ: Again, you colour Ògún
too much with your mouth.
Olohun-iyo, I warn you
Praise them, not fight the battle
with your mouth.
Olohun-iyo, I warn you.

VOICE: That was what my father taught me.
I only say what my father taught me.
I am Olohun-iyo
with a tongue coated in honey
drenched with the power to intoxicate
I sing in the way my father taught me.
Do I offend you, my lord?

ÈSÙ: Just be warned, you may loose a few teeth on what
your father did not teach you. Ògún Onire, I call you.

*(Again amidst the cheers of the crowd, the drums
change to Ògún's music. A group of Ògún Ijala hunters
step forward dancing the dance of Ògún. Ògún joins
them amidst greater cheers. Ògún dances wildly. The
crowd as with the case of Sàngó join, Èsù not too happy
at the cheers of Ògún, steps forward)*

Oti to!
My two great friends are here.
The prize to be won is here also

I call on the warriors to prepare
themselves for battle.

(Sàngó and Ògún prepare themselves for battle. The Egunguns return. Charms are won by both fighters. Dane guns are shot. Songs are sung. Amidst all the noise, the two fighters ready to do battle step forward. The crowd take sides and stand on the side of the warrior they want to cheer. As the fighters face each other ready for the clash, Yemoja rises from her stool. She steps forward)

YEMOJA: Òrúnmìla o
The great wise one, My lips can not remain firm, watch all this dust thrown around me. Ògún takes my love beyond me and brings it to the market square to sell me cheap in the eyes of many. Now his temper blurs my emotions and allows the senseless take hold of his manly wits. I shall not be the prized bull of these men. Oh no, I won't.

Òrúnmìla my father
The dust of these men carry the stain of shame leaving the sour taste on my lips. Before Olodumare, I am innocent.
And yet before your eyes … I hate to think what you think I am.
Therefore, I shall leave you all to the intrigues of your minds.
To a place where I shall be an egg whose yoke shall be the key to life
I shall today step into the big blue sea answering to the different needs of all who call me Yemoja, Emanja, Orisa n'la.

(The Iyaji comes forward with the eight priestesses)

IYAJI: Yemoja o
  Yemoja o
  Emanja o
  As you step into the sea
  You become one with it
  Emanja o
  As those with different tongues call you
  You become the true goddess of all
  Yemoja, yeye-ọmọ-eja
  Sege si i, awura-olu
  Ẹyẹ Orungan
  Àgbà òòsà tí í wẹ'mọ 'è láwèyè
  Ọ́ lọ́mi tùtù nlé, we'mo e lawemo
  Òòsa odo tí í da gójógójó
  Awogba arun mo gb' eje
  Olówó eyo, Aje Saluga
  Òòsà tí í f' wórò ojó w'ẹmọ 'è láwèyè
  Òòsà tí ń gbé 'nú ibú solá
  Yemoja o
  Yemoja o
  Emanja o
  Òòsà odò tí í bú
  Yeriyeri molote.

  Yemoja, go where you will
  If when we call, you shall answer
  the cries of your children.
  Yemoja, go where you will
  But remember home always
  Yemoja go where you will
  And when you are dressed differently,
  Or adored differently

Cr adorned differently
We, shall remember in turn
that Yemoja belongs to all of us now.
Yemoja, gba mi o

CROWD: Bá wá wò tiwa

IYAJI: Yèyé àgàn, gbà mí o

CROWD: Bá wá wo tiwa

(As the song continues in a slow sway Yemoja dances off into the sea. The Cuban song takes over in slow sway. Four young male slaves tied together, and four young female priestesses accompany and sing the song as Yemoja sways into the sea.)

SONG: Emanja Apetu
Apetu Emanja

Emanja Apetu
Apetu Emanja

Emanja Olodo
Olodo Emanja

Ralamawa
Emanja Olodo
Olodo Emanja

Olomo wewe ye mi o
Emanja Apetu
Apetu Emanja

Emanja Olodo
Olodo Emanja

IYAJI: Be happy, be merry,
Our mother has not left us.

Yemoja is with us always!

(A wild tempo takes over. The other hero-gods retire quietly as the crowd dances and sings in honour of Yemoja. As they dance off the stage, spotlight on the masked face of the little dancer. She turns to the audience and watches as the procession dances off the stage. She joins the dancers as final lights fall on the shrine of Yemoja. The lights hold for a while and go off slowly into final darkness.)

The End

www.ingramcontent.com/pod-product-compliance
Lightning Source LLC
Chambersburg PA
CBHW020709270326
41928CB00005B/347